CONTENTS

Finding out about dinosaurs   4

Dinosaur fossils   6

What do fossil hunters do?   8

Where does Simon look for fossils?   10

Simon finds a fossil   12

What tools does Simon use?   14

Studying a footprint   16

Studying a skull   18

What happens to the fossils?   20

Thinking and talking about dinosaurs   22

Activities   24

Finding out about dinosaurs

Dinosaurs lived a long time ago.

There were many different kinds of dinosaur.

This is a picture of one of the first dinosaurs.

Eoraptor
ee-o-rap-tor

Hunting For Dinosaurs

by Leonie Bennett

Consultant: Dougal Dixon

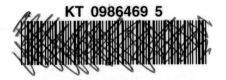

Copyright © **ticktock Entertainment Ltd 2007**
First published in Great Britain in 2007 by **ticktock Media Ltd.,**
Unit 2, Orchard Business Centre, North Farm Road, Tunbridge Wells, Kent TN2 3XF

We would like to thank: Shirley Bickler and Suzanne Baker

ISBN 978 1 84696 610 1 pbk
Printed in China

Picture credits
t=top, b=bottom, c=centre, l-left, r=right, OFC= outside front cover
Lisa Alderson: 4; Robin Carter: 13; Corbis: 5, 8-9, 18b, 22b; Luis Rey: 17, 19;
Shutterstock: 1, 7, 10, 11, 12, 14b & t, 15, 16, 18t, 20-21, 21t, 22t, 23t, 23c, 23b.

These men try to find out about dinosaurs.
It is their job. They are fossil hunters.

Fossil hunters

Dinosaur fossils

We learn about dinosaurs by looking at fossils.

Fossils are the bones of dead animals. They are so old that they have turned into stone.

This is the fossil of a dinosaur skull.

What do you think this dinosaur liked to eat?

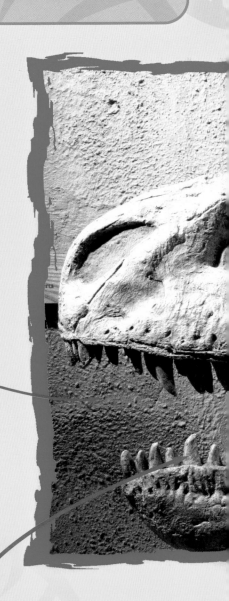

Lots of sharp teeth

Big eyes

Strong jaws

This dinosaur had sharp teeth. We can tell that it was a scary hunter.

What do fossil hunters do?

This is Simon. It is his job to look for fossils.

Simon looks for fossils in rocks.

He digs the fossils out of the
rock very carefully.

Rock

Hammer

Where does Simon look for fossils?

Fossils are found in lots of places.

Some fossils are found on the beach.

Beach

Some fossils are found in rocky mountains.

Mountains

Fossils have been found all over the world.

Simon finds a fossil

When Simon finds a fossil, he uses a brush to clean it.

Brush

Fossil

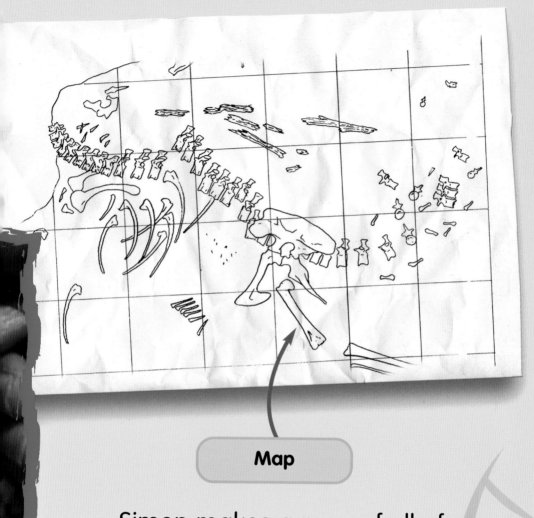

Map

Simon makes a map of all of the fossils he finds.

He writes down what it is and where he found it.

What tools does Simon use?

Simon uses a hammer
to get the fossils out
of the rock.

He uses very small brushes
to clean sand and dirt from
the fossils.

Fossil hunters also use computers to find out about dinosaurs.

Studying a footprint

Simon can tell a lot from this footprint.

Dinosaur footprint

The dinosaur that made it was very big. It walked on three toes.

Simon thinks it was an Iguanodon.

Iguanodon ate plants. It was about ten metres long.

Iguanodon
ig-wan-o-don

Three toes

Studying a skull

Simon found this dinosaur skull.
It is very big!

The dinosaur had big
sharp teeth.

Teeth

Tyrannosaurus rex
tie-ran-o-sor-us rex

Sharp teeth

Simon thinks it was
a T. rex.

19

What happens to the fossils?

Most fossils go to museums.

The museum puts the fossils together.

They put the dinosaur skeleton in a room.

Apatosaurus skeleton

Apatosaurus
a-pat-o-sor-us

The museum tells us about the dinosaur.

Now everybody can find out more about dinosaurs!

Thinking and talking about dinosaurs

What is a fossil made of?

- Stone

- Bone

- Mud

What does Simon use to dig out a dinosaur fossil?

Name the places that a fossil might be found.

What might be the best thing about looking for fossils?

What kind of dinosaur does Simon think this fossil is?

Activities

What did you think of this book?

 Brilliant   **Good**   **OK**

• • • • • • • • • • • • • •

Make a sentence with these words:

toes. • had • Iguanodon • three

• • • • • • • • • • • • •

Would you like to be a fossil hunter?
Why?

• • • • • • • • • • • •

Who is the author of this book?
Have you read *Amazing Dinosaur Facts* by the same author?